DUFFIELD BRANCH LIBRARY
2507 WEST GRAND BOULEVARD
DETROIT, MICHIGAN 48208
(313) 481-1712

LINDA RICHARDSON BROWN

ISBN 978-1-64003-940-7 (Paperback)
ISBN 978-1-64003-941-4 (Digital)

Copyright © 2018 Linda Richardson Brown
All rights reserved
First Edition

All rights reserved. No part of this publication may be reproduced, distributed, or transmitted in any form or by any means, including photocopying, recording, or other electronic or mechanical methods without the prior written permission of the publisher. For permission requests, solicit the publisher via the address below.

Covenant Books, Inc.
11661 Hwy 707
Murrells Inlet, SC 29576
www.covenantbooks.com

To my grandchildren, Corde' Bonner
and Aaliyah Bonner-Jones.

"Colin, what's wrong? Why do you look so sad?"

That's what Grandma asked me as we drove away from the school. Why won't the words come out of my mouth? I was bullied today.

Michael Beano likes to pinch, punch, and kick. When we are on the playground, he punches me. When we are in class sitting at the desk, he kicks me.

When we are standing in line he pinches me. I hate school. I don't want to go back. Not tomorrow. Not ever. Instead I say, "Nothing Grandma".

It's another school day. Another day with Michael Beano.
Ring! Ring!
I heard the sound of the school bell. I walked slowly into class and sat down at my desk.

"Colin!" I jumped when Mrs. Scott called my name for attendance. "Colin, are you with us? I called your name three times."

I wanted to say, "No, I'm not with you all. I feel alone. I feel lost. I feel like crying inside. I feel sad. I feel bad about myself." But instead, I said, "Present."

I looked around the class, and I saw Michael Beano staring at me. I wanted to melt away and disappear.

Almost every day that was how my school day went. I was too afraid to tell the teacher or my parents about Michael Beano bullying me. I sat in my class, not talking to anyone, hoping the school day would end fast.

Thinking about playing with my sister and video games when I got home from school helped me get through the day. Although, thinking about things other than my schoolwork always got me in trouble, and poor grades were at the top of the list.

Ms. Scott was always busy when Michael Beano would pinch me. If I was at the back of the line, Ms. Scott was at the front of the line leading the class. If I was kicked sitting at my desk, Ms. Scott was writing on the chalk board. If I was punched on the playground, Ms. Scott thought we were playing.

One day at the playground, I thought about the words Grandma would have me speak in front of the mirror in the mornings when getting ready for school: "I feel good about myself. I am smart. I am brave. I am confident. I believe in myself."

She told me to always believe those words. I decided to tell Grandma about Michael Beano. I'll never forget that day.

The next day while in class, Michael Beano was sent to the principal's office. He was told there was no bullying and to keep his hands to himself. The principal also called his parents. Michael Beano promised to leave me alone. Just like that, I was free to be me.

Ms. Scott told the class that we were all made differently and no one was made the same. Tall or short, big or small, quiet or not, we were all human beings and deserved to be treated with respect.

Ring! Ring!

I heard the sound of the school bell. I walked into class and sat at my desk.

"Colin?" Ms. Scott called my name for attendance.

Today, with a smile on my face, I raised my hand, and I said, "Present."

Discussion Questions

1. What is bullying?
2. How did Colin feel when he was bullied?
3. If you are bullied, what should you do?
4. If you see someone being bullied, what should you do?
5. Do we all look alike?
6. Should we bully kids who look different from us?
7. Why do you think Colin didn't tell he was being bullied?
8. Why is bullying wrong?
9. Can you name some things that will make you feel good inside?
10. Why is it important to tell an adult if you or someone else is bullied?

I Am Worksheet

Fill in the blanks.

Example: I am brave.

1. I am _____
2. I am _____
3. I am _____
4. I am _____
5. I am _____
6. I am _____
7. I am _____
8. I am _____
9. I am _____
10. I am _____

About the Author

Linda Richardson Brown is a licensed practical nurse who lives in Metro Detroit. As a student of life and life coaching, she pursues a second career as a life empowerment coach. *Free To Be Me* was birthed because of her grandson verbally shutting down in school because of bullying. Linda Richardson Brown hopes that this most important story serves as a voice for all victims who have fell silent and is used as a tool for children everywhere, teaching educators and parents the possible signs of bullying.

CPSIA information can be obtained
at www.ICGtesting.com
Printed in the USA
BVHW022350220119
538240BV00001B/2/P